1

Table of Contents

Glossary of Acronyms

ACLU	American Civil Liberties Union
BJS	Bureau of Justice Statistics (under DOJ)
CRCL	Office for Civil Rights and Civil Liberties (under DHS)
CRD	Civil Rights Division (under DOJ)
CRS	Community Relations Service (under DOJ)
DHS	United States Department of Homeland Security
DOJ	United States Department of Justice
EEOC	United States Equal Employment Opportunity Commission
EU	European Union
FBI	Federal Bureau of Investigation (under DOJ)
ICCPR	International Covenant on Civil and Political Rights
ICCT	Incident Community Coordination Team
ICERD	International Convention on the Elimination of All Forms of Racial Discrimination
NGO	Non-governmental Organization
ODIHR	Office for Democratic Institutions and Human Rights (under OSCE)
OHCHR	United Nations Office of the High Commissioner for Human Rights
OIC	Organization of Islamic Cooperation
OSCE	Organization of Security and Cooperation in Europe
TSA	United States Transportation Security Administration
UNGA	United Nations General Assembly
UNHRC or HRC	United Nations Human Rights Council
USCIS	United States Citizenship and Immigration Services (under DHS)

Executive Summary

At the invitation of Secretary of State Hillary Clinton, representatives of 26 governments and four international organizations met in Washington, D.C. on December 12-14, 2011 to discuss the implementation of United Nations Human Rights Council Resolution (UNHRC) 16/18 on "Combating Intolerance, Negative Stereotyping and Stigmatization of, and Discrimination, Incitement to Violence and Violence Against, Persons Based on Religion or Belief." In her closing remarks, Secretary Clinton stressed, "The United States is hosting this conference because religious freedom and freedom of expression are among our highest values. They are enshrined in our Constitution. For people everywhere, faith and religious practice is a central source of our identity. It provides our lives with meaning and context. It is fundamental to who we are."

The implementation meeting focused on two elements of the steps set forth in Resolution 16/18: 1) prohibiting discrimination based on religion or belief and 2) training government officials, including on how to implement effective outreach to religious communities. Participants agreed that their task was to keep the discussion focused on implementing the specific steps called for in Resolution 16/18, rather than broadening the dialogue to other possible measures not included in the resolution.

Presenters and participants in the interactive sessions were law enforcement and anti-discrimination experts. Presenters included experts from invited countries and international organizations, as well as personnel from the United States Departments of Homeland Security and Justice.

Discussions were held under "Chatham House Rule" in order to promote a free and candid exchange of views. Accordingly, while this report reflects accurately the points made and best practices described by all participants, approval was sought before attributing specific remarks to particular participants.

The sessions produced a rich exchange of best practices, which are set forth in the body of this report. Key conclusions for policy makers include the following:

1. Participating countries already have in place legal prohibitions of discrimination and violence based on religion or belief. While the nature of these prohibitions vary – some are contained in national constitutions, others in domestic laws, and still others in international instruments that have the same importance in the relevant countries as domestic law – there does not appear to be a fundamental gap in the domestic legal framework of the majority of participant countries.

2. Many countries have specialized units in their justice ministries or prosecutor general's offices which have proven effective in imposing civil, and at times criminal, penalties against those found to have engaged in violence or discrimination on the basis of religion or belief in employment, the provision of public services, or in access to public accommodations such as hotels and restaurants. Others rely on regular prosecutors to enforce these laws. Civil enforcement of anti-discrimination laws has proven to be the

most effective and is most widely used. Strong public outreach is a key factor in all systems. Effective outreach not only ensures that the population knows authorities are willing and able to take on religious discrimination cases, but also teaches citizens how to call such cases to the attention of authorities.

3. There is a wide variation in training for government officials. Some countries have specialized programs focused on training officials to consider religious sensitivities when formulating and implementing policies and practices; others have no specific training in this area.

4. The disparity in training is reflected in wide variations in the systematization of outreach to religious communities. Some countries have highly structured outreach systems. These systems ensure that communities are aware of potential or actual changes in policy that may affect them, the rationale behind such policies, and the opportunity that communities have to shape such policies through their input. Other countries do not have a systematic way of conducting such outreach, but many have developed creative and effective ad hoc methods for such engagement.

5. Effective national security policy and protection of human rights are mutually reinforcing. Law enforcement needs the cooperation of religious and other communities to fight violent extremism. Communities will not cooperate if they perceive that their members are being discriminated against or that their members' beliefs are not being respected by the authorities. Extremists can use such perceptions to further their own ends. Profiling based on religion or ethnicity not only violates human rights, but also provides a false sense of security and allows actual terrorists to proceed undetected.

PLENARY SESSION I: Comparative Legal Frameworks Prohibiting Discrimination and Crimes of Violence on the Basis of Religion or Belief in Participant Countries

Description: In this opening plenary session, participants presented an overview of their domestic legal frameworks for prohibiting discrimination and crimes of violence on the basis of religion or belief.

Presentations Overview:
The presentations provided details of the legal mechanisms available for governments and private citizens to protect against discrimination on the basis of religion or belief, as well as potential limitations in the existing frameworks. Participants generally had such provisions operative in their legal systems through some combination of the following mechanisms: their constitution, specific legislation, court precedent related to prohibitions on discrimination, and the transposition of international instruments such as the International Covenant on Civil and Political Rights (ICCPR) into their domestic legal systems. Given the prevalence of these legal provisions, their effective enforcement was seen as more pressing than the need to adjust extant legal frameworks. This opening exchange set the stage for more detailed discussions on effective enforcement strategies and practices throughout the proceedings.

European Union: The presentation of the European Union (EU) noted that EU primary law establishes a legal framework against discrimination on the basis of religion or belief. These sources of law include the European Convention on Human Rights and the EU Charter on Fundamental Rights. There are also several relevant EU treaties, including the Treaty on the European Union and the Treaty on the Functioning of the European Union. The main secondary law in the EU on this issue is the Racial Equality Directive of 2000 and the Employment Equality Directive of 2000. The Employment Equality Directive allows limited exceptions to the principle of equal treatment, e.g., in the case of hiring by a religious organization. There is a proposal for a new directive on discrimination on the basis of religion or belief (and several other grounds) outside the context of employment.

Organization of Islamic Cooperation: In July 2011, OIC Secretary General Ihsanoglu and Secretary Clinton co-chaired a High-Level Ministerial on Implementing Resolution 16/18 in Istanbul. EU High Representative for Foreign Affairs Ashton and Ministers of Foreign Affairs and representatives from 20 nations attended the ministerial. The goal was to encourage governments to implement Resolution 16/18 in order to address the issue of intolerance, discrimination, and stigmatization on the basis of religion or belief. The OIC looked forward to the international community addressing these important issues and reiterated commitment to the resolution, which refers to key points made by the OIC Secretary General in Geneva in 2010. The United Nations General Assembly (UNGA) Third Committee's adoption of a similar resolution was a step forward. Resolution 16/18 and the joint statement in Istanbul call for common action to implement the resolution. The OIC expressed appreciation for Ambassador Johnson Cook's statement and those of the Department of Justice (DOJ) and the Department of Homeland Security (DHS) on United States policies. The OIC noted that there were some differences in the nature and scope of the legal framework presentations. Some countries noted the importance of international law. The OIC further stressed that the nexus between freedom of expression and freedom of religion or belief needs to be clarified. The OIC believes that the Istanbul Process can help with this, and that if undertaken on a consensual basis, the implementation process will yield positive results.

The OIC Secretary General welcomed the United States initiative to hold the first expert level meeting and underscored that the process was focused on consensual implementation of HRC Resolution 16/18. His message noted that the success of the alternative approach contained in Resolution 16/18 will be judged by addressing vital concerns of all in a time bound framework. As mentioned in the resolution, steps to end double standards and racial or religious profiling ought to be taken. The OIC Secretary General further stated that Resolution 16/18 provided a good basis for concerted action by states, at both the national and the international levels and must be utilized accordingly.

Other participants that delivered remarks included: *Belgium, Brazil, Canada, Chile, Czech Republic, Egypt, Germany, Indonesia, Jordan, Malaysia, Netherlands, Nigeria, Norway, Poland, Sweden, Turkey, United Arab Emirates, United Kingdom, and the United States.*

Key Points Made:
- Almost all participants have constitutional protections for freedom of religion or belief, equal protection of the law and nondiscrimination.

- Many participants have domestic legislation in place that prohibits discrimination on the basis of religion or belief.
- Some participants incorporate international law directly into their domestic legal systems, or model their domestic laws on international law.
- Many participants have laws providing individuals or civil society groups with the private right of action to sue government and private entities for discrimination.
- Many participants allow government entities to bring cases against individuals or entities for discriminatory practices.
- A number of participants have independent commissions or ombudsman offices to independently investigate discrimination and bring cases forward, liaise with civil society groups and community members about such issues, and help disseminate relevant information regarding legal protections and duties.
- Many states have criminal law provisions for enhanced sentencing consideration for crimes motivated by religious animus, and some states also have criminal law sanctions for various acts of discrimination.

PLENARY SESSION II: Roundtable Demonstration: Engagement with Religious Minority Communities in the United States

Description: A participant from the Office for Civil Rights and Civil Liberties (CRCL) at the United States Department of Homeland Security (DHS) described his office's responsibility to protect the United States from foreign and domestic threats while guaranteeing that the protection of national security is carried out without infringing upon constitutional freedoms. DHS/CRCL relies on a number of tools to accomplish this mission, including regular engagement with diverse ethnic and religious communities in cities across the United States. This session familiarized participants with DHS/CRCL's engagement process and set the stage for subsequent discussions of engagement strategies. Participants had the opportunity to witness a re-creation of a community engagement roundtable where community stakeholders raised civil rights concerns with DHS personnel. Meeting participants were also able to ask questions of the community stakeholders and DHS personnel to propose suggestions and best practices of their own.

Presentation Overview:
One DHS participant indicated that DHS consistently meets with diverse organizations representing many communities across the United States interested in homeland security issues. According to this participant, DHS regularly invites participation by new stakeholders and advocacy organizations. Community engagement roundtables allow participants to address grievances and government agencies to share information about government programs and procedures with community stakeholders. The agendas for roundtable discussions are finalized in advance of the meeting and in coordination with government and community representatives. Feedback and information learned from roundtables is provided directly to DHS senior leadership.

The DHS participant continued by elaborating on the goals of the roundtable process. These include: reaching broader audiences, providing access to community events, and obtaining information about community interests and concerns. DHS/CRCL roundtables have helped assure that communities have accurate information about government policies and practices, both by conveying information to the representatives and by identifying gaps in public information.

Participants from a diverse set of religious communities, civil rights advocates, and participants from the United States Department of Homeland Security, and the Department of Justice, engaged in a roundtable discussion with representatives of various religious and faith-based communities as well as civil rights and civil liberties groups.

Roundtable Demonstration:
A roundtable participant expressed concern over the perception that the United States Transportation Security Administration (TSA) (a component agency of the Department of Homeland Security) was selecting individuals for extra screening at airports on the basis of racial, religious, or ethnic profiling. The DHS/TSA participant expanded that DHS policy does not condone profiling on the basis of race, religion, or national origin in any area, including airport screening. Making presumptions based on race, religion, or national origin has also been shown to be ineffective in protecting security, as it draws resources away from other potential threats. United States screening procedures use profiles based on behavior and specific intelligence about the activities of extremist groups.

Roundtable participants stated that there are increased security checks for refugees coming from Muslim-majority countries. This has significantly hindered the refugee resettlement process, and participants wondered if this violates individuals' religious freedom. According to the DHS participant, new interagency refugee checking procedures do cause delays. These delays, however, apply equally to all refugees, regardless of nationality. There is no discrimination against Muslims or persons from Muslim-majority countries. All refugees, irrespective of national origin, routinely submit to background checks. Work is underway to reduce these delays.

Post-Roundtable Discussion:
One participant from a European country noted that the perception of the Sikh community abroad is different from that in the United States. He asked one participant in the roundtable if the Sikh community in the United States reaches out to schools and universities to build an understanding about the Sikh community.

The roundtable participant responded that for the last two years, the Sikh community has worked with the state of Texas on an effort to incorporate information on Sikhs into the state's social studies curricula. The community was successful in persuading the Texas Board of Education. This was significant because Texas represents the largest textbook market in the United States, and thus textbooks approved by Texas are widely used across the country. The Sikh community also uses mass media and entertainment. For example, the clothing company Kenneth Cole promoted public awareness using a Sikh model. In addition, the Sikh community also seeks to counter the perception that it is trying to distance itself from Muslim communities.

DHS participants added that the United States government has conducted a number of presentations to law enforcement agencies, DHS personnel, and other United States government personnel after September 11, 2001 on Sikh religious practices and traditions. The DHS/CRCL office also has a number of training materials, including videos and posters, concerning Sikh traditions and sensitivities that are used by various United States agencies and the wider public.

One country participant noted that some countries have expressed concern about allowing individuals who manifest their religion, for example through religious dress, to serve in publicly visible capacities. The United States participant responded that the United States government is prohibited by law from discriminating on the basis of religion. Many employees in the United States are permitted to express their religion through dress provided that it does not interfere with their job performance. The federal government must also provide accommodation to individuals who demonstrate a bona fide belief, including days off for religious observance, prayer times, etc.

Another country participant asked if DHS/CRCL consults communities before introducing a new policy. DHS participants responded that there have been instances where DHS consulted with communities prior to introducing a new policy. Whether to do so is determined largely on a case-by-case basis. Roundtable participants noted resentment can be fostered when communities are not consulted. In these cases, communities use other tools to encourage the administration to change policies, including lobbying Congress and engaging the public to put pressure on the administration.

Key Points Made
- The goals of a community engagement roundtable include: reaching broader audiences, providing access to community events, and obtaining information about community interests and concerns.
- Trust-building, frank discussions, and regular engagement are critical for ongoing community support. Non-governmental participants believe engagement is more productive when undertaken prior to making a change in policy or practice.
- Community engagement roundtables are more effective when recommendations from participants are reviewed by senior government leadership.
- Continued engagement by the United States government, particularly DHS with religious and civil liberties communities, is essential to a national security policy that not only is mindful of human rights but also is understood and accepted by those communities.
- Religious communities can lobby federal and local levels of government, reach out to private enterprises, and engage the public through mass media in order to advocate for fair legislation and law enforcement practices.
- Community consultation helps lay the groundwork for more effective implementation of new policies and regulations.

ENFORCING ANTI-DISCRIMINATION LAWS INTERACTIVE SESSION I:
Preventing Religious Discrimination by Government Actors: Laws prohibiting religious discrimination by government agencies and employees: zoning and land use, public employment, discrimination in public education, religious profiling by law enforcement

Description: This session provided an overview of how governments use laws to prevent religious discrimination by government actors. The session focused on legal frameworks and strategies for combating discrimination on the basis of religion or belief in areas such as public employment, public education, zoning and land use.

Presentation overview:
A Department of Justice (DOJ) participant from the Civil Rights Division (CRD) explained its role to enforce United States anti-discrimination laws, including laws which prohibit discrimination on the basis of religion. The DOJ/CRD uses civil law penalties as opposed to criminal sanctions for the majority of its anti-discrimination work. The DOJ/CRD takes enforcement action against state and local government actors in areas such as housing, lending, employment, education, public accommodations, public facilities, construction of places of worship and religious schools, and the prison system. As part of the federal government, the DOJ/CRD cannot bring actions against federal entities, but private citizens can bring such cases. Fee-shifting provisions in the civil rights laws, which provide for the recovery from defendants of prevailing plaintiff's attorneys' fees and costs, make it easier for citizens to obtain an attorney to bring those types of cases. In addition, federal agencies have independent inspector generals who monitor, among other things, discrimination-related issues.

The DOJ/CRD participant noted that most actions result in settlements negotiated between the DOJ/CRD and the state or local government entities accused of discrimination. These settlements typically take the form of consent decrees, which are filed with a court and remain under court jurisdiction for several years. If a settlement cannot be reached, the DOJ/CRD will proceed with a lawsuit, and can obtain injunctive relief, in which a court orders changes to the defendant's conduct and/or monetary compensation.

This participant continued, pointing out that in the workplace, religious discrimination cases often arise when employers refuse to make "reasonable accommodations" for employees' religious practice, some of which involve dress codes that prohibit employees from wearing religious clothing. DOJ provided examples of cases that were settled successfully by changing employer practices, such as the 2010 case of a New Jersey county that did not allow a jail official to wear a headscarf. With the involvement of DOJ, the employer changed its practices. Reasonable accommodation issues also arise with regards to time off for employees for religious activity; DOJ obtained a settlement in such a case in Illinois on behalf of a teacher who requested sufficient leave to attend a religious pilgrimage.

In the area of education, the DOJ/CRD participant highlighted DOJ involvement in cases relating to religiously motivated discrimination and harassment. Such cases have included the right of Muslim girls to wear headscarves to school, the right to be absent for religious holidays, and the right of students to assemble for religious activities during free time at school.

According to the DOJ/CRD participant, the Department also helps to combat housing discrimination in accordance with the Fair Housing Act. Discriminatory land use decisions involving places of worship are brought under the Religious Land Use and Institutionalized Persons Act, a statute which ensures that religious groups are not discriminated against by local authorities in building religious facilities.

One country's independent equality ombudsman also presented its model for combating public discrimination on the basis of religion or belief. The participant explained that criminal law in his country, which applies to both private and public actors, prohibits religious discrimination. However, it is rarely used and is generally ineffective because under criminal law, guilt and discriminatory intent must be proven beyond a reasonable doubt. The government thus tends to use civil law more often. These laws also apply to both public and private actors. When using civil law, there is a lower burden of proof and courts need only look at the effect of the alleged discriminatory act, without having to show intent. With regards to enforcement, the ombudsman can take cases to court, which is important in enforcing the law and highlighting important issues. Individuals can also bring cases themselves. The ombudsman cannot seek injunctive relief, but only monetary compensation.

This country participant noted a few difficulties in combating discrimination. One such difficulty is that not all of society is covered. The judiciary, for example, is not covered by the anti-discrimination laws. Furthermore, where discrimination is not overt, it is difficult to bring cases. The participant noted he would prefer to see broader laws to address all areas where law enforcement and public bodies are active.

Discussion:
Participants from several countries and international and regional organizations contributed to the follow-up discussion. Most, but not all, countries stated that they had civil anti-discrimination laws; some felt religious discrimination was not often found in their societies. Other participants discussed their own legal frameworks, including whether the discrimination laws apply to public and private actors, whether to use civil or criminal law, and which part of the government is best suited to enforce such laws. Canada and other participants discussed the scope of their discrimination laws; many countries' laws extended to areas such as housing and employment, though some also covered delivery of goods and services. Participants gave examples of cases in which their governments or their independent bodies brought cases and the importance of strategic litigation to educate society.

Participants also discussed the utility of government mediation as a tool to complement legal action. Participants noted the difficulty in educating society about non-discrimination and human rights. One country participant highlighted its success in using non-governmental actors, such as religious institutions, to spread such a message. A United States participant noted the importance of outreach and dialogue with community leaders, emphasizing that enforcement of the law itself fosters cultural sensitivity.

Key Points Made:
- The scope of anti-discrimination laws varies, but tends to include housing, employment and education. In some cases, delivery of services and goods, prison systems, and land use are also covered. Laws tend to cover public authorities, and in many cases private actors as well.
- Government agencies cannot be relied upon to police themselves; entities independent of the governmental actor under scrutiny are essential. In unitary systems, an independent office of human rights or an ombudsman is a viable system. In a federal system, the federal government can effectively enforce the law against state and local governments.

In cases where the system relies on individuals to bring enforcement action, some form of cost shifting may help to mitigate the resource imbalance between an individual and a government agency. However, many participants thought it essential for either an independent body or the government to bring such cases and not to rely solely on the limited resources available to individuals.

- Most countries with anti-discrimination laws that are both civil and criminal prefer to use civil laws. Civil laws have a lower burden of proof and are more effective in combating discrimination.
- Litigation has to be used strategically and as a last resort; other tools such as education and mediation can be just as effective. In many cases, an administrative system is easier for individuals to access, operates more quickly, costs less, and offers a useful alternative to litigation. Litigation is most useful when it can change practices and educate society.

ENFORCING ANTI-DISCRIMINATION LAWS INTERACTIVE SESSION II:
Preventing Religious Discrimination by Private Actors: employment discrimination, housing discrimination, discrimination in places of public accomodations, and similar forms of discrimination by businesses and other private entities

Description: This session explored legal tools and frameworks for preventing and addressing discrimination by non-governmental actors, particularly in the areas of housing, private business employment discrimination, and equal access to public accommodations. The discussion highlighted tools available to both private actors and government entities to address discrimination by non-government actors.

Presentation Overview
A participant from the United States Department of Justice (DOJ) gave the initial presentation of United States law on this topic. The United States Constitution bars discrimination by state actors, while separate statutes bar discrimination by private actors. The 1968 Fair Housing Act, for instance, prohibits discrimination on the basis of race, religion, or other protected classifications. In the housing context, DOJ sometimes tests implementation by sending out housing "applicants" who differ only by race or religion to ascertain whether they are treated differently when they seek to purchase or rent housing.

The DOJ participant indicated that the law regarding public accommodations applies to food establishments, lodging establishments, and places of public entertainment. Most states' anti-discrimination laws apply to any business open to the public, including small businesses. DOJ can receive complaints on these issues, or it may learn about allegations of discrimination from the media. DOJ reviews cases and has authority to file suit in the name of the United States to vindicate individual rights.

Regarding employment, the DOJ participant pointed out that the United States Equal Employment Opportunity Commission (EEOC), a separate law enforcement agency focused on enforcing federal employment law, receives approximately 100,000 complaints of employment discrimination per year. Race discrimination allegations account for the largest share, at approximately 36,000. In recent years there have been approximately 4,000 cases of religious discrimination brought per year.

The DOJ participant continued by discussing issues relating to the conflict between religious freedom and equal employment rights with respect to religious employers. In general, religious organizations have certain exemptions from relevant anti-discrimination laws. Religious institutions can properly include an individual's religion as a qualification for employment, and can decide whether all or only some employees must be of that religion. This also applies to charities that are deemed "ministries." A more difficult question arises regarding whether religious organizations are exempted from laws that prohibit discrimination on the basis of other categories, such as gender or ethnicity. United States courts have exempted religious organizations from such laws in regards to their hiring of ministers or other officials who conduct religious services or activities.

According to the DOJ participant, Title VI provides that groups receiving federal funding may not discriminate on the grounds of race, national origin, or ethnicity. Religion is not included, but many individual funding programs have bars on religious discrimination. Also, religious and ethnic discrimination can overlap, so the ban on national origin discrimination may cover some of these cases.

Discussion:
Participants from several countries and international and regional organizations contributed to the follow up discussion.

Several participants noted that testing for discrimination (by sending otherwise similarly qualified applicants of differing race or religion) was also used in their countries; others were unsure whether such programs would be lawful in their countries. There was much discussion on the issue of hiring by religious organizations. Many participants have laws that exempt religious organizations from religious discrimination provisions, but such exemptions are limited by principles of proportionality and necessity. The issue of religious accommodations in the employment context was also heavily discussed. Some participants provided examples of cases involving both private and public sector employers in which courts ordered that employees be allowed to wear religious dress or take religious observance days. Others noted that there were some exceptions recognized in the law for such accommodations for religious dress, including health and security.

Key Points Made
- Almost all of the participants who spoke noted that discrimination by private actors in housing, employment, and public accommodations is unlawful. Some have special units in their governments to enforce these provisions, some rely on regular government prosecutors, and still others rely on individuals to bring actions in court.
- Government action to address discrimination in the private sector, including the filing of court cases, is an important complement to private rights of action to sue for discrimination. Systems relying solely on private action are not as successful in combating discrimination.

- Investigations by the government to uncover discriminatory practices, including the use of testing activities, can be an effective tool for law enforcement.
- Religious organizations should be exempt from certain discrimination law provisions to allow for particular hiring practices.
- Accommodations for religious beliefs and practices, including dress and grooming, is an important issue in the private sector. Some countries seek, either through legislation or court decisions, to require employers to allow such practices; others, however, have barred public displays of religious dress/symbols in an effort to avoid interfaith friction.

ENFORCING ANTI-DISCRIMINATION LAWS INTERACTIVE SESSION III:
Prosecuting Crimes of Violence Motivated by Religion or Belief (Hate Crimes)

Description: This session addressed criminal laws against violence and threats of death or bodily injury based on religion or belief.

Presentation Overview:
A participant from the Organization of Security and Cooperation in Europe's (OSCE) Office for Democratic Institutions and Human Rights (ODIHR) discussed his office's mandate to collect data on hate crimes and to publish an annual hate crimes report. His office has a number of tools to assist governments in prosecuting hate crimes including a guide on drafting legislation in this area. They have also produced a guide for NGOs to work on these issues. Two additional practical guides will be published soon, one on prosecuting hate crimes, and the second on gathering data on hate crimes. OSCE/ODIHR provides hate crimes related training for civil society prosecutors and law enforcement. The OSCE/ODIHR participant discussed issues his office encounters. For instance, it is not always possible to judge whether there is only one bias behind the crime or a combination of biases, which can lead to complications for data collection as the same crime can be recorded across multiple statistics for multiple grounds. With regards to data collection, he discussed the importance of disaggregated data and the problem of underreporting due to reluctance or fear on the part of victims. He also discussed the importance of flexible legislation which allows prosecutors to prosecute both the underlying offense and also the hate crime. Thus if the bias motive cannot be proven a conviction can still be obtained.

A DOJ participant presented the United States perspective on this issue. United States federal law classifies violent crimes against the person, crimes against property, and "true threats" when they are motivated by racial, ethnic or religious bias as "hate crimes". Until 2009, United States federal law made hate crimes actionable only if the victim was engaging in certain federally protected activities such as voting, employment, education, housing, using public accommodations, acting as a juror, or using interstate commerce. In 2009, Congress enacted a new law prohibiting certain violent crimes motivated by racial, religious, or other specific biases, regardless of any connection to a federally protected activity.

The DOJ participant pointed out that aside from violent crimes against individuals, federal hate crimes law also covers damaging property because of its religious characteristics. The federal government investigates and prosecutes cases involving arson and destruction of churches, mosques, synagogues, and other places of worship. The third category of hate crimes, "true threats," are communications made through words, gestures, or symbolic speech intended to cause fear of death or bodily injury. The communication has to be a threat to an individual, as bigoted speech in and of itself is not unlawful.

Discussion:
Participants from several countries and international and regional organizations contributed to the follow up discussion. These participants identified a wide variation in practice; some countries have hate crimes laws and others rely on generally applicable criminal law to prosecute crimes motivated by religious bias. Even among those countries that do have hate crimes legislation, there was wide variation as to how those laws are implemented, with some having specialized independent units and others relying on regular prosecutors. Suggestions on how to give this issue greater attention included hosting legislative debates and web campaigns in order to increase awareness and encourage victims to file complaints with the police.

Participants discussed the bases of bias for hate crimes. A hate crime is motivated not by the perpetrator's response to the victim's behavior, but rather by his or her response to the victim's characteristics, such as religion and race. In this context, the discussion centered on which characteristics should be considered under hate crime legislation. Some hate crime laws covered crimes arising from bias based on race, religion, sex, disability, sexual orientation, and national origin. Others included categories such as age or political opinion. In Canada and some other countries, the list was open and left to court discretion.

In a number of countries, participants highlighted difficulties with filing complaints based on hate crimes legislation. An additional problem is posed by a lack of awareness on the part of law enforcement personnel. Country participants agreed that greater efforts to educate both law enforcement and the public at large are required. It was noted that while hate crimes are committed against individuals or their property, they are inherently intended as an attack on entire segments of society, and therefore negatively affect society as a whole.

There was some discussion of differences between hate speech and hate crimes. Resolution 16/18 calls for action in the case of the latter, where an actual crime against individuals or property is involved.

Participants agreed that accurate data collection is important both to help legislators shape hate crime laws and to help law enforcement determine whether policies designed to reduce violence based on religion or belief are having their intended effect.

Key Points Made:
- Hate crime laws are important even if the underlying acts have already been criminalized. Enhanced penalties for bias-motivated crimes send a message to society that hate crimes affect more than just individual victims, and therefore negatively affect society as a whole.
- Many, but not all, participant countries have enacted hate crime laws. Some were separate statutes while others captured the notion by including bias motives as an aggravating factor for enhanced sentencing in hate crime cases. Some participants considered the latter approach more straightforward.

- There is a need for greater awareness and capacity building for victims (who often do not report these crimes), civil society, law enforcement, and the judiciary. Regional organizations can assist with training in this regard.
- Hate crime laws should offer prosecutors sufficient flexibility to pursue cases with mixed motives and to prosecute either the bias-motivated crime or the underlying crime if the bias motive cannot be proven.
- Hate crime laws should also protect those without a religious belief such as atheists.

ENFORCING ANTI-DISCRIMINATION LAWS INTERACTIVE SESSION IV: Metrics and Complaint Mechanisms: Measuring the Effectiveness of Law Enforcement

Description: This session explored systems for gathering data on instances of religious discrimination and religion-based hate crimes, as well as for evaluating the success of governmental efforts to counter them.

Presentation Overview:
A participant from the United States Department of Justice (DOJ) provided the opening presentation on this topic. The primary data collection tool used by DOJ is the Federal Bureau of Investigation's (FBI) annual Hate Crimes Statistics report. The report is mandated by the 1990 Hate Crimes Statistics Act. The collection mechanisms were developed by the FBI in consultation with a number of civil society groups. The report is available to the public on the Internet, and the data include criminal offenses motivated either in whole or in part by certain biases. The data is only based on reported crimes and comes from the voluntary cooperation of law enforcement agencies, currently about 17,000 agencies covering 95% of the United States population. It is part of the DOJ's Uniform Crime Reporting data-collection program, which covers all crimes and is also available on the web.

The DOJ participant stated that the Hate Crimes Statistics report covers bias motivation relating to eleven types of crimes, including murder, manslaughter, rape, robbery, arson, motor vehicle theft, and others. The DOJ Bureau of Justice Statistics (BJS) periodically analyzes the hate crimes data and works with local agencies to improve reporting. The DOJ/BJS also periodically polls a nationally representative sample of households on crime victimization, which allows for estimates of the likelihood of victimization based on a number of victim characteristics. In June 2011, DOJ/BJS issued a special report on hate crimes between 2003 and 2009, which captures incidents and victims whether they were reported to law enforcement or not. Victims' reports were corroborated to the extent possible with police records. The DOJ/BJS report, however, does not measure murders or crimes against persons under 12. Other agencies also collect relevant data. The Equal Employment Opportunity Commission (EEOC), for example, tracks religious discrimination in employment.

According to the DOJ participant, these data collection methods have some shortcomings. The FBI report is based on voluntary participation, and also relies on law enforcement agencies to be accurate in classifying their data. In addition, the report only captures reported hate crimes; the DOJ/BJS report indicates that half of all hate crimes are not reported. The DOJ/BJS report has shortcomings too, in that it is an extrapolation based on relatively small samples, and relies on the victim's perception of the perpetrator's motivation.

The DOJ participant continued by saying despite shortcomings the benefits of this methodology and data collection is numerous. First, the data and methodology are public and inform law enforcement, policymakers, and civil society of relevant proportions and trends. The information allows NGOs to increase awareness in the community and determine how to better address needs. It also helps government determine where to allocate resources and how to improve laws.

Discussion:

Participants from several countries and international and regional organizations contributed to the follow up discussion, which primarily focused on data collection methodology and techniques. Participants agreed that data collection is a critical feedback mechanism to inform good policymaking and to alert both government and the public at large to trends and the state of the status quo. A participant noted that data collection is also useful in reporting to international organizations, but only 30 percent of states comply with reporting to United Nations (UN) treaty bodies, thereby weakening their effectiveness.

Participants identified particular bodies that are charged with collecting data, usually in cooperation with regional authorities, and issuing reports for the country. Participants noted that underreporting was a common problem. Several participants noted the importance of working closely with civil society organizations, as they are close to the communities and can help encourage reporting. Several participants said that they use surveys to help remedy underreporting. Surveys can help to reveal general attitudes and discrimination concerns that would not otherwise appear in data based solely on reported cases. Disaggregated data broken down along the lines of locality and type of crime was seen as most useful.

Several participants noted that through the media, people can be better informed of their rights, the various legal protections available to them, and means of redress for grievances.

Key Points Made
- Consistent and recurring crime data collection and reporting informs law enforcement officials, policymakers, and civil society groups of facts and trends in order to assess the effectiveness of existing policies and programs and to help allocate resources and attention to the most pressing issues.
- It is important to engage civil society organizations in crime data collection and reporting policy to ensure that local concerns are addressed and that communities are aware of and contribute to the programs.
- Publicly available data that is disaggregated on the basis of locality, crime committed, and bias motivation is most effective in informing relevant law enforcement officials, policymakers, and civil society organizations.
- Surveys are an important tool in helping to compensate for the underreporting of crimes.
- In conducting any data collection activity, it is important to protect sensitive personal information to ensure that victims are comfortable in reporting crimes.

- Dissemination of crime metrics and data helps to engage and inform the public of these important issues.

ENFORCING ANTI-DISCRIMINATION LAWS INTERACTIVE SESSION V: Limitations and Challenges to Enforcing Anti-Discrimination Laws

Description: This session explored areas in which participant states believe they face the greatest challenges, areas where there may be gaps in domestic protection, and where they believe the greatest challenges will be in the future.

Presentation Overview:
One country participant began this session by discussing his government's recent experience with enacting a law to protect against discrimination on the basis of religion. In drafting the law, the government examined its obligations under the International Convention on the Elimination of All Forms of Racial Discrimination (ICERD) and the International Covenant on Civil and Political Rights (ICCPR). His government's challenge was to ensure freedom of expression while taking measures against discrimination. He noted that prohibitions under Article 20 have to be compatible with Article 19 of the ICCPR. He mentioned that while some United Nations (UN) initiatives did address the issue of incitement, many states remain divided. He welcomed the cooperation demonstrated by participant governments in putting aside unresolved issues and agreeing to Resolution 16/18.

A participant from the Civil Rights Division (CRD) at the United States Department of Justice (DOJ) then discussed some of the challenges his office faces in its work. He noted that in the United States, one short-term challenge is the 50 percent increase in hate crimes directed at Muslims in 2010. This is notable particularly after a period of steadily declining rates of hate crimes against Muslims in the years following September 11, 2001 "9/11." He also reported a recent increase in land use disputes involving mosques. He noted that DOJ does not want this to become a long-term problem, and the United States government is bringing resources to bear on this issue. The United States participant noted that a participant country mentioned the challenge of prohibiting advocacy of national, racial, or religious hatred that constitutes incitement to discrimination, hostility, or violence, as provided for in Article 20 of the ICCPR without infringing freedom of expression as guaranteed under Article 19. The United States approach involves only barring "true threats" and incitement to imminent violence, but does not bar other types of speech. The United States believes more speech is the answer to offensive speech. For detailed United States views on Article 20 please see
http://www.ohchr.org/Documents/Issues/Expression/ICCPR/States2011/USA.pdf

The participant from the European Union (EU) then gave a presentation discussing the challenges his organization sees. The EU has had an employment equality directive in place for over a decade. It includes religion as a protected characteristic, and is binding on member states. However, members still need their own legislation to direct the means and methods of enforcement. The European Commission can bring action against member states who do not comply with the directive. The provision of the EU directive which exempts churches and religious organizations in regards to employment discrimination has also been difficult to implement at the national level. The conflict between dress codes and manifestation of religion through dress is still controversial in the employment context. The EU participant noted that another challenge is dissemination of information on anti-discrimination and social dialogue on related issues. Accessing justice and realizing the protections afforded by these legal provisions for victims is also difficult. In this regard, victims struggle with finding access to legal aid and short time limits in which to bring a case forward. These are areas in which equality bodies can perhaps offer support. The EU participant also emphasized that governments also need to look at other tools such as training programs, cultural dialogues, and youth action programs to combat discrimination.

Discussion:
Participants from several countries and international and regional organizations contributed to the follow up discussion, which focused on recent European Court of Human Rights decisions that have addressed issues in this field. Challenges discussed included limited resources for equality bodies, lack of awareness of rights and responsibilities, creating a culture where anti-discrimination enforcement is understood, and lack of access to justice.

Key Points Made:
- While it can be challenging to enact comprehensive and useful laws with regards to anti-discrimination, a larger challenge can be creating awareness of such laws and how individuals can use them. In this vein, changing societal attitudes can also be a challenge. Participants recognized the role equality bodies, NGOs, community leaders, government entities, and media can play in this area.
- Limited resources for governmental/equality bodies can also pose a challenge. In this regard, empowering civil society by providing funds for it to bring cases, increased legal aid services, and using tools other than litigation such as education and outreach can all be effective in combating discrimination.
- Participants noted that an increase in awareness as well as an increase in resources are both necessary so that victims can access legal services on their behalf.

GOVERNMENT OUTREACH AND TRAINING INTERACTIVE SESSION I:
Community Engagement and Outreach: Models for good governance in addressing grievances, informing policy, and facilitating understanding

Description: This session discussed outreach models and tools that respond to community concerns and provide information on government programs, activities, and issues. The goal of these measures is to build trust and establish a routine process for communication and coordination with diverse community leaders and organizations.

Presentation Overview:
The United States Department of Homeland Security (DHS) participant explained that the United States government has many goals in engaging civil society. One is to communicate reliable information about federal programs and policies directly to community leaders. Another is to obtain feedback from the community regarding concerns and the impact of government programs. This feedback can only come through relationship building, and can be accomplished

through roundtables, monthly e-newsletters, and subject matter policy consultations. The DHS participant provided examples of substantive policy consultations such as listening to the concerns of a range of faith communities with regard to airport screenings, modesty concerns specific to the images generated by body scanners, and privacy concerns about what is to be done with those images. As a result of these consultations, additional protections and enhanced communications were implemented to respond to concerns and protect security.

According to the DHS participant, the Departments of State, Commerce, Education, Health and Human Services, and Treasury all implement similar tools as part of their outreach and engagement to civil society groups, including faith-based communities. The Incident Community Coordination Team (ICCT) team at the Department of Justice uses a conference call method to receive feedback from community leaders following national security incidents. DHS has a complaint form for persons who believe they have been victims of profiling, even if by private security officers; it is meant to address individual concerns and make sure policy addresses civil liberties.

A Canadian participant introduced Canada's relevant policies. Canada's outreach is focused on intercultural and interfaith dialogue. Since 1971 the Government of Canada has had a specific government policy on multiculturalism that celebrates and promotes diversity in order to remove barriers to the full social, economic, and civic participation of Canadians of all origins. This policy is enshrined in legislation (*The Canadian Multiculturalism Act*, 1988) and the Constitution (through section 27 of the *Canadian Charter of Rights and Freedoms*). Provincial and territorial governments in Canada have also adopted multiculturalism policies and legislation that mirror the objectives of the federal approach. The policy, together with government funding for various programs that promote social cohesion, have contributed to Canadians' positive attitudes toward immigration and an openness to diversity. In cooperation with the Canadian Race Relations Foundation (www.crr.ca), the Government of Canada is currently creating a national, interfaith council to address issues related to increasing religious diversity.

According to the Canadian participant, the Canadian Department of Public Safety's Citizen Engagement Division leads outreach to ethno-cultural communities on issues related to national security and public safety. In 2004, a cross-cultural roundtable on security was created to engage Canadians in a long term dialogue about national security issues. The roundtable consists of fifteen members, who are social and cultural leaders from diverse communities with varying viewpoints on the discussion topics. The role of the roundtable is to advise Public Safety and Justice Ministers on the impact of national security policies and programs. The Division also uses a hands-on approach to engage youth, with activities such as being witnesses in mock crimes and assuming the role of customs officer. These interactions provide two-way communication in that it helps communities understand and trust government while enhancing awareness of community concerns by government officials.

Discussion:
One participant noted that dialogue is very important because people generally value engagement with their government. Therefore an individual approach, including personal contact with communities, is important both in formal and informal settings. This country does not have a formal roundtable process; however, delegations from various departments and agencies

occasionally gather and visit with communities. The participant emphasized creating contacts individually and to develop a credible relationship. Another participant noted that it maintains an open and transparent dialogue with religious communities that began more than twenty years ago.

Key Points Made:
- Governments should communicate information about programs to community leaders as well as obtain feedback from communities about ongoing concerns and the impact of those programs.
- To accomplish these goals, governments may utilize roundtables, monthly e-newsletters, subject matter policy consultations, conference calls with community leaders, and complaint forms. These are all viable mechanisms of outreach and engagement with civil society.
- Youth engagement is also important. Activities such as witnessing mock crimes and assuming the role of customs officers help youth to gain awareness of diverse community concerns and build positive attitudes.

GOVERNMENT OUTREACH AND TRAINING INTERACTIVE SESSION II:
Government engagement with communities in conflict

Description: This session discussed how best to deal with communities in which a sizeable segment perceives themselves or other members of their community to be alienated from or in conflict with the rest of the society. Sometimes for immigrant communities these conflicts are extensions of real armed conflicts occurring in their countries of origin. The presentation focused on conflict and grievance resolution mechanisms available at the federal, state, and local levels. The session also addressed effective practices for successful engagement with communities in conflict. Such practices include the development of local capacity to prevent hate crimes and to address tension associated with allegations of discrimination.

Presentation Overview:
A participant from the United States Department of Homeland Security (DHS) presented on the United States model, reiterating President Obama's point that freedom in America is indivisible from the right to practice one's religion. Almost all states in the United States have civil rights laws and DHS strives to ensure that communities know that their members have rights and should not be afraid to exercise them.

The DHS participant noted that the United States endeavors to engage with faith communities and minority communities, especially those in which members feel alienated. Such engagement has four objectives: communication of reliable information to the public about available programs, redress of grievances, reception of feedback, and promoting integration and trust among communities. Promoting integration and trust can be challenging, especially in communities that lack experience dealing with the government. Advocacy organizations can be safeguards against the erosion of human rights.

The DHS participant continued by stating that after the terrorist attacks of 9/11, the United States Government embarked on a robust engagement with Muslim, Middle Eastern, South East Asian, and Sikh communities, through their community leaders and advocacy organizations. However, it is difficult for the government to engage newer (immigrant/refugee) communities when mature advocacy organizations are not present. In addition, prior negative experiences with government and law enforcement agencies in other countries make these communities suspicious of government in general and cause them to avoid any interaction with authority.

The DHS participant expanded on this point with the example of the Somali-American immigrant community in the United States. The United States government has taken particular care to engage with the Somali-American immigrant community for the past three years in an effort to prevent domestic violent extremism and protect the civil rights and civil liberties of the community. Discussions not only focus on security, but also on social services and United States policy toward their country of origin. This dialogue encouraged Somali-American community groups to organize youth summits and conferences to discuss violent extremism, the community's role in protecting national security and the protection of civil liberties. In order to earn the trust of minority groups and faith based communities, it is found particularly effective for governments to share information with the public, seek feedback on policies and programs that may impact particular communities, stay responsive to community needs, and address fears by treating particular communities as equal partners.

A participant from the United States Department of Justice's (DOJ) Community Relations Service (CRS) talked about other resources that the government can offer to help communities address conflict peacefully. While other parts of the DOJ enforce civil rights laws in the United States, DOJ/CRS works with communities in conflict to address tension associated with allegations of discrimination by facilitating dialogue, providing training, and conducting mediation. Examples include facilitating communication between people organizing protests and law enforcement officials as well as providing training to help keep protests safe and reduce the potential for violence. DOJ/CRS also works with communities on strategies to prevent and respond more effectively to violent hate crimes. In the aftermath of hate crimes, DOJ/CRS has worked with diverse community members to facilitate the kinds of dialogues and activities that allow communities to recognize commonality in a way they may not have been able to before. DOJ/CRS also works with local community leaders to conduct training on cultural professionalism and offers technical assistance before, during, and after major events, protests, or vigils. This gives communities a chance to engage positively with law enforcement and demonstrates to law enforcement how dedicated community members are to investing their time and energy into creating a safer community.

The DOJ/CRS participant stressed that his office intervenes when its services are requested, and sometimes on its own initiative if need be. The mediation agreements produced during this process are not legally enforceable, but parties may choose to issue a public statement outlining their shared commitment to take certain remedial action. DOJ/CRS conciliators are required under United States law to conduct their activities in confidence, without publicity, and are prohibited from disclosing confidential information. The participant from DOJ/CRS explained that in his experience, if an event occurs in the United States or overseas that may lead to tension in the United States, engaging early and discussing the issue with the relevant community or communities is important.

According to the DOJ/CRS participant, the SPIRIT Program, an American program which stands for Student Problem Identification and Resolution of Issues Together, engages students and stakeholders in formulating solutions to school conflicts. It identifies issues of concern and provides a process through which students develop potential solutions. Invariably, groups of diverse backgrounds identify similar issues of concern. The students and stakeholders then develop solutions and action plans to improve their school environment, as well as a report that details the actions all parties commit to take. The program aims to develop a culture in schools and communities to mediate conflict and develop lines of communication in a peaceful and productive way.

Another participant presented on methods in her country to alleviate community conflict. Though there are dozens of ethnic groups and languages in her country, the national ethic emphasizes the unity of all citizens. Despite this successful policy of creating a strong national identity, conflict still exists.

This participant noted that ethnic conflicts also sometimes take on religious tones. For example, one city in her country has seen violence apparently motivated by religion, such as the burning of mosques and churches. However, deeper analysis showed the issue had to do with the exercise of political rights. Christians from this city and Muslims who have come there to settle have both been there for years. Some local officials assert that more recent arrivals were not natives of the area and therefore not entitled to exercise political rights there, but the participant noted that this is a misinterpretation of their constitution. Under their constitution, a person born in an area is a native of that area regardless of his ancestors' place of origin. The participant noted that because free speech may be used to create more conflict, the government often appeals to the media to encourage and educate people and avoid aggravating dangerous situations.

According to this country participant, police are the first key law enforcement agents. When an individual trains as a police officer, he or she enlists as a citizen of the country, not as a member of a religious or ethnic group. Police have a mandate to protect everyone, not just those from a certain geographic region or religious or ethnic group. However, law enforcement must be sensitive to religion or belief. There is standardized training to recognize the needs of a community. The police have a community relations committee made up of all key stake-holders. The goal of these committees is to encourage unity. For example in this participants country, the president observes religious holidays that are not his own to demonstrate unity.

The participant emphasized that a crime in her country is not a crime against a Muslim or Christian, but a crime against the laws of the country.

Discussion:
A Canadian representative noted that Canada strives to engage citizens, particularly youth, through social media.

When asked about the immigration experience for Somalis, a United States participant responded that conflicts arise because of differences in worldviews, education, and culture. Somali-Americans have experienced smoother integration due to support structures within their communities. Throughout the history of the United States, immigrant communities have experienced similar circumstances. The language barrier can also contribute to significant misunderstandings. Post 9/11, members of some Muslim communities including Somalis have faced certain challenges.

The United States participant pointed out that training youth leaders is the most effective way to reach rural communities. Teaching them methods of conflict resolution and allowing them to observe their own communities through group discussions has proven to be an effective model. Successful cases have led to youth working with government officials to find solutions to particular community conflicts.

One participant noted that his country has a large community of Somali refugees, and that the prejudices towards the community were based more on cultural or political ignorance than on the basis of religion.

A United States participant pointed out that it is important to engage new immigrants so they can learn about culture, practices, and social norms of the United States. Creating a safe and resilient community requires all pieces, including civil society, local partners, local outreach, etc.

Key Points Made:
- Building a sense of common national identity is important and requires a sustained effort by leaders throughout society.
- In order to earn the trust of minority groups and faith based communities, it is found particularly effective when governments share information with the public, seek feedback on policies and programs that may impact particular communities, stay responsive to community needs, and address fears by treating particular communities as equal partners.
- Conflicts apparently based on religious differences can be motivated by political considerations. In order to mitigate conflict, leaders should understand the underlying issues and devise a strategy to address the drivers of particular conflicts.
- Social media and new technologies can be effectively harnessed to engage the youth of communities in conflict.
- Citizens organizing peaceful protests should be encouraged to communicate with law enforcement officials before the protest date in order to keep the event safe.
- Training on cultural sensitivities for community leaders and technical assistance before, during, and after major events, protests, and/or vigils will provide communities a chance to engage positively with law enforcement. This also demonstrates to law enforcement officials that community members are dedicated to creating safer communities.

GOVERNMENT OUTREACH AND TRAINING INTERACTIVE SESSION III:
Preventing and alleviating state discrimination based on religion or belief

Description: This session examined the means by which governments can ensure that state agents respect the rights of individuals, including their right to freely worship. Participants had the opportunity to discuss how respect for diverse religious observance, dress, and conduct may be taken into account in the formulation of national security policy.

Presentation overview:
A United States Department of Homeland Security (DHS) Office for Civil Rights and Civil Liberties (CRCL) participant presented on his office's work with civil society, NGOs, and a wide range of demographic groups and law enforcement agencies across the country.

According to the DHS participant, domestic implementation of anti-discrimination laws is an integral part of the national security plan. The United States participant noted that security measures cannot be implemented successfully without the understanding and support of religious and ethnic communities. For example, there is no monolithic "Muslim community" in the United States; there are diverse Muslim communities and the government needs to respect that diversity. Discussions must include the participation of representatives from business, civil rights, religious, and community leaders, as well as leaders of professional organizations. Similarly, religious freedom abroad cannot be advanced if it is not protected at home.

The DHS participant described some of the religious-sensitivity training programs for DHS officials. For example, during the Hajj season, a training course for Transportation Security Agency (TSA) personnel teaches them to advise passengers to put holy water in their checked bags because if it is over three ounces, it will be confiscated. No policy is changed, but this training can have a great impact.

Three challenges to inter-religious communication were identified by the DHS presenter: 1) combining inter-religious communication with an appreciation for intra-religious diversity without reinforcing intra-religious hierarchies and including women in these communications, 2) involving smaller religious groups in established projects, and 3) maintaining conceptual inclusiveness concerning government roles.

Discussion:
One country participant stated that his country's constitution guarantees freedom of speech and the right to express views in public and through the media within the boundaries of the law. He observed that when freedom of expression involves religion and creed, criticisms should be constructive to safeguard national unity. The participant's country recently passed legislation to protect equal opportunity, and to guarantee rights for all members of society. A committee of Christians and Muslims in the participant's country facilitates inter-religious dialogue and responds immediately if problems arise. The participant suggested that countries should enlist the assistance of clergy to remove any misunderstandings. The objective of the participant's current legal reforms are to establish that religions and creeds are respected, that members of all religions should be dealt with as individual citizens and not distinguished based on religion, gender, or faith. They are also committed to protecting religious rights and freedom of expression.

A country participant discussed that coordination between concerned authorities, houses of worship, the press, and other interested parties to promote peace and tolerance would facilitate interfaith cooperation. An international exchange between countries with expertise in training would also be helpful.

According to a Canadian participant, Canada is developing toolkits to enable grassroots organizations to undertake interfaith dialogue and organize into vehicles for social change. This may also be a way for civil society groups to work together and to engage more youth. Another country participant suggested that dialogue must take place on equal footing to encourage action.

Key Points Made:
- Stringent security measures must be balanced by respect for ethnic and religious groups, so that such measures are not perceived as directed against specific communities.
- The effectiveness of security measures is greatly enhanced by the active support and participation of diverse community representatives.
- Countries may enlist the assistance of clergy to remove any misunderstandings and facilitate dialogue between the government and religious communities.
- Grassroots organizations can also play a positive role in promoting interfaith dialogue and encouraging social change.
- Governments should encourage cooperation between concerned authorities, houses of worship, the press, and other interested parties to promote peace and tolerance.

GOVERNMENT OUTREACH AND TRAINING INTERACTIVE SESSION IV: Immigration Enforcement and Civil Rights

Description: This session explored immigration enforcement policy, the civil rights and civil liberties protections afforded to those detained in immigration proceedings, and policies affecting other migrants. Included was a discussion of how civil rights protections are integrated into border security policy.

Presentation Overview:
According to a participant from the Department of Homeland Security (DHS), the United States 1964 Civil Rights Act includes protections against discrimination based on national origin. At the same time, the United States Government lifted some immigration restrictions that mostly allowed immigrants from Europe into the country. The Civil Rights Act is credited with creating a more open environment, which facilitated tremendous growth in immigration, which peaked during the 1990-2000s. This foreign born population generally belongs to one of three groups: naturalized citizens, legal permanent residents, and undocumented immigrants. Civil rights protect all persons in the United States, including undocumented immigrants, against abuse. In practice, however, this is challenging because these immigrants may be less willing to approach authorities.

The DHS participant pointed out that the immigrant population in the United States has grown steadily since the 1960s; today 40 million Americans are foreign born. Immigration has also fostered religious diversity. Faith-based organizations are at the forefront of immigration issues at the national and local levels. They also provide language classes and other services vital to immigrant communities. A large population of immigrant children and youth is a focus of community work, particularly through interfaith efforts. When an issue of discrimination arises with a particular immigrant community, DHS policy is not to relocate individuals as a conflict mitigating measure. In such instances, DHS undertakes community engagement efforts through the United States Citizenship and Immigration Services' (USCIS) 21 district offices and 81 field offices throughout the country.

According to the DHS participant, the DHS/USCIS prepares new immigrants for life in the United States through such initiatives as the publication of a guide for new immigrants and a website called *WelcometoUSA.gov*. In addition, the DHS/USCIS recently launched a Citizenship Awareness Initiative with targeted public service advertisements to raise awareness about the naturalization process. The campaign also offers a Citizenship Resource Center with information and study tools. The DHS/USCIS also manages a grant program that funds non-profit organizations to help immigrants prepare for the citizenship process. Public libraries are one of the many local institutions that help immigrants adjust to life in the United States. They play a critical role in the integration of immigrants. The DHS/USCIS also has an Office of Public Engagement to assist in immigrant integration.

The DHS participant emphasized his organization's extensive work with immigrant communities. Through roundtables and other events, immigrant and civil rights advocacy groups (such as the American Civil Liberties Union (ACLU)), have advocated for the human rights of immigrants.

Discussion:

One country participant asked if there is a minimum standard of knowledge, understanding, and attitude necessary to become a naturalized citizen. The United States participant noted procedural and residency requirements, including requirements on how long an individual must have lived in the United States in order to be naturalized. There are also moral character evaluations, criminal background investigations, a basic English language test (which can be exempted in the case of age), and a basic test of United States history and the values and principles reflected in the United States Constitution and Bill of Rights.

Another country participant asked what policies apply to immigrants fleeing catastrophes in their home countries. The United States participant responded that there is a temporary status program for individuals fleeing catastrophes or other situations that would make it dangerous for them to return to their country. If granted temporary status, they are allowed to stay in the United States until conditions improve.

One country participant posed a question on how countries provide outreach to immigrants. The DHS participant responded that his office works through a variety of means such as foundations, foreign born organizations, and charity organizations that support the immigration process and help provide information to the government and civil society. A Canadian participant also remarked that his government provides approximately $900 million annually to non-governmental settlement organizations that provide services to newcomers in their first 3-5 years in Canada (in the areas of language training, information and orientation services, and labor market preparation, for example).

Key Points Made:
- Legislation to protect against discrimination on the basis of national origin and religion is essential to encouraging immigration and successfully integrating immigrant communities into their new countries.
- Relocation of immigrants away from geographical areas where they experience discrimination does not address underlying issues of intolerance and hatred; it is more effective to conduct community engagement to resolve concerns.
- Resources such as pamphlets, educational classes, websites, and DVDs can be effective tools in helping immigrants integrate.
- Government funding for non-profit organizations focused on settling new immigrants is another viable integration method.
- Roundtables led by government agencies can serve as mechanisms to address the perceptions and concerns of new arrivals and thus help agencies formulate policies to protect the human rights of immigrants.

GOVERNMENT OUTREACH AND TRAINING INTERACTIVE SESSION V: Demonstration of Training United States Government Officials

Description: This session provided an overview of the training that the Department of Homeland Security (DHS) delivers on cultural competency for DHS and law enforcement personnel while preserving freedoms guaranteed by the United States Constitution. Topics included misconceptions and stereotypes regarding religious communities; a how-to guide for community interaction; how effective national security policing requires avoidance of the use of ethnic or religious profiling; and the United States Government approach to engagement and outreach.

Presentation overview:
A DHS participant presented the United States model of law enforcement training. Essentially, police cannot be effective without the cooperation of local communities. Local communities will not cooperate if they believe the police are discriminating against them based on their ethnic or national origin or on the basis of their religion or belief. The DHS participant noted that after September 11, 2001, there has been a focus on groups such as Muslims, Arabs, Sikhs, South Asians, and Somalis.

The DHS participant noted that the education of law enforcement officers about specific religions can alleviate misunderstandings. DHS provides, for example, training on misunderstandings about Muslims in the United States. Muslims have been in the United States for longer than most non-Muslim Americans believe, and Muslim immigrants tend to be more integrated than other immigrants. Only three percent of the United States Muslim population has been in the United States for less than ten years. Law enforcement officer training emphasizes the importance of charity in Islam and highlights the Quranic principles of justice, dignity, and mercy. The training emphasized that prayer is important to many Muslims and should not be viewed as threatening. After September 11, 2001, the United States government designed a training program to educate law enforcement personnel specifically about the Hajj. Trainees were taught to address airport security in a culturally sensitive manner, particularly during times when large numbers of Muslims travel, many with containers of holy water.

According to the DHS participant, there is a perception by some Muslims that they cannot speak out against the United States government and that their rights are different than those of others. Law enforcement not only needs to avoid feeding this perception lest the false narrative be used by extremists, but also has an affirmative duty to counter it. Thus, it is the role of the government to teach law enforcement officials to make clear in speech and practice that everyone's rights are equal and that views and opinions in and of themselves are not illegal.

The DHS participant pointed out that in order to build safe and resilient communities, the United States government focuses on civil rights enforcement by reaching out to religious leaders, civil society, and local partners. It also conducts competency training for law enforcement officials. The United States is starting to use a range of metrics to evaluate the impact of these training courses.

The DHS participant also emphasized that racial or religious profiling does not help ensure security from a law enforcement standpoint. Security threats come from many sources and this type of profiling alienates individuals while overlooking other threats. During the DHS presentation, the group was shown a law enforcement training video. The video shown to the group included a "spot the terrorist" segment in which pictures of a wide variety of persons of differing races, ages, ethnic background, and genders, often wearing different religious symbols were shown. At the end of the film it was revealed that every one of the individuals shown had been a terrorist; any effort to have distinguished among them based on these characteristics would have resulted in a terrorist threat being overlooked.

The DHS participant cautioned that if data is compiled only by law enforcement agencies, there may be discrepancies. Community surveys can fill these gaps. Such data can serve as a social mirror and be used for strategic litigation. It is important to post the data collection results online.

According to the DHS participant, the United States seeks to address its ongoing challenges by striving to pass robust laws and focusing on uniform implementation of the law. Training law enforcement and empowering civil society to be a part of enforcement mechanisms increases access to justice for victims.

Key Points Made:
- It is critical to establish trust and community relations before problems arise, so that communities can assist and not hinder law enforcement efforts.
- Terrorists and other threats to security can come from any background. Focusing only on specific religious or ethnic backgrounds does not enhance national security, and stereotypes members of minority groups. Racial or religious profiling is not effective from a law enforcement perspective.
- Training on religious minorities for law enforcement officials can increase cultural sensitivity, help overcome stereotypes, and more effectively protect national security as well as civil rights.
- The more the government can educate, break down stereotypes, and increase dialogue, the more understanding and the less fear there will be between law enforcement and

citizens, and the more cooperation there will be in combating those who actually do pose a threat of violence.

Annex

Closing Remarks by Secretary of State Hillary Rodham Clinton, Wednesday, December 14, 2011

Well, good afternoon, everyone, and I want to thank you all for participating in this conference where we are working together to protect two fundamental freedoms – the right to practice one's religion freely and the right to express one's opinion without fear.

I'm delighted to see so many members of the diplomatic corps. I welcome all of you here to the State Department. I especially wish to acknowledge Ambassador Suzan Johnson Cook, who has been leading our efforts, and also Ambassador Eileen Donahoe, the United States Ambassador to the Human Rights Council, who has also been tireless in pursuit of America's fundamental and the world's universal values.

Now this year, the international community in the Human Rights Council made an important commitment. And it was really historic, because before then, we had seen the international community pit against one another freedom of religion and freedom of expression. And there were those in the international community who vigorously and passionately defended one but not the other. And our goal in the work that so many nations represented here have been doing, with the adoption of Resolution 1618 and then again last month in the General Assembly's Third Committee, was to say we all can do better. And this resolution marks a step forward in creating a safe global environment for practicing and expressing one's beliefs. In it, we pledge to protect the freedom of religion for all while also protecting freedom of expression. And we enshrined our commitment to tolerance and inclusivity by agreeing to certain concrete steps to combat violence and discrimination based on religion or belief. These steps, we hope, will help foster a climate that respects the human rights of all.

Now, the United States is hosting this conference because religious freedom and freedom of expression are among our highest values. They are enshrined in our Constitution. For people everywhere, faith and religious practice is a central source of our identity. It provides our lives with meaning and context. It is fundamental to who we are. And as the Universal Declaration of Human Rights makes clear, each of us is born free to practice any religion, to change our religion, or to have none at all. No state may grant these freedoms as a privilege or take them away as a punishment if you believe, as I do and as our country does, that they are not rights bestowed by any government. They are rights endowed by our Creator within each of us. And therefore, we have a special obligation to protect these God-given rights.

And if a government does try to deny them or take them away, it amounts to a rejection of that universal right. And it also amounts to a repudiation of that fundamental conviction that we are all created equal before God. Therefore, restricting the practice of anyone's faith is a threat to the human rights of all individuals. Communities of faith are not confined by geopolitical borders. Wherever you are in the world, there will certainly be people whose religious beliefs differ from your own, maybe by just a little bit or maybe by a lot. And my ability to practice my religious faith freely does not, and indeed cannot, diminish yours.

Religion can be such a powerful bond, but we also recognize that it can be misused to create conflict. There are those who, for reasons actually having little to do with religion, seek to instill fear or contempt for those of another creed. So we believe that it is the duty of every government to ensure that individuals are not subject to violence, discrimination, or intimidation because of their faith or their lack of faith. That is the commitment that the world made to religious freedom more than 60 years ago when we adopted the Universal Declaration of Human Rights.

At the same time, as we strive to protect individuals from violence and discrimination because of their religion or their beliefs, we must also express the freedom of expression. Now, in the United States, we take that especially seriously because many of those who came to our country came for religious reasons. They came because they were being discriminated against or their religion was being outlawed. They started coming in the 17th century, and they still come all the way through the 21st century.

Well, how would one know that you were being discriminated against if you didn't have the right to freedom of expression? Your neighbor knows, well, that person is different from me because he or she believes differently. So the freedom of religion and the freedom of expression are absolutely bound up together.

Now, there are those who have always seen a tension between these two freedoms, especially when one person's speech seems to question someone else's religious beliefs, or maybe even offends that person's beliefs. But the truth we have learned, through a lot of trial and error over more than 235 years in our country, is that we defend our beliefs best by defending free expression for everyone, and it lowers the temperature. It creates an environment in which you are free to exercise and to speak about your religion, whether your neighbor or someone across the town agrees with you or not. In fact, the appropriate answer to speech that offends is more speech.

Now, in the United States, we continue to combat intolerance because it is – unfortunately, seems to be part of human nature. It is hurtful when bigotry pollutes the public sphere, but the state does not silence ideas, no matter how disagreeable they might be, because we believe that in the end, the best way to treat offensive speech is by people either ignoring it or combating it with good arguments and good speech that overwhelms it.

So we do speak out and condemn hateful speech. In fact, we think it is our duty to do so, but we don't ban it or criminalize it. And over the centuries, what we have found is that the rough edges get rubbed off, and people are free to believe and speak, even though they may hold diametrically opposing views.

Now, with Resolution 1618, we have clarified these dual objectives. We embrace the role that free expression plays in bolstering religious tolerance. We have agreed to build a culture of understanding and acceptance through concrete measures to combat discrimination and violence, such as education and outreach, and we are working together to achieve those objectives.

Now, I know that in the world today, intolerance is not confined to any part of the world or any group of people. We all continue to deal with different forms of religious intolerance. That's true here, that's true in Europe, that's true among countries in the Organization of Islamic

Cooperation, everywhere in the world. It's true where people, if they are discriminating or intimidating, they're doing it against Muslims or Jews or Christians or Buddhists or Baha'is or you name it. There has been discrimination of every kind against every religion known to man.

And yet at the same time, it's one thing if people are just disagreeing. That is fair game. That's free speech. But if it results in sectarian clashes, if it results in the destruction or the defacement or the vandalization of religious sites, if it even results in imprisonment or death, then government must held those – hold those who are responsible accountable. Government must stand up for the freedom of religion and the freedom of expression. And it's a situation which is troubling to us, because a recent study by the Pew Forum on Religion and Public Life found that 70 percent of the world's population lives in countries with a high number of restrictions on religious freedom.

In America, we are proud of our long and distinctive record of championing both freedom of speech and freedom of religion, and we have worked to share our best practices. But I have to say we have one difficulty in understanding all of the problems that we see around the world, and that is that because religion is so personal and because it is something that we highly value in ourselves, it strikes us as troubling that people are not confident in their religious beliefs to the point where they do not fear speech that raises questions about religion.

I mean, every one of us who is a religious person knows that there are some who may not support or approve of our religion. But is our religion so weak that statements of disapproval will cause us to lose our faiths? That would be most unfortunate. In fact, what we have found, in study after study, is that the United States is one of the most religious countries in the world. And yet anybody can believe anything and go anywhere. And so there is no contradiction between having strong religious beliefs and having the freedom to exercise them and to speak about them and to even have good debates with others.

And so the United States has made a commitment to support the 1618 implementation efforts, but we also would hope that we can take practical steps to engage with members of religious minority groups. We know that antidiscrimination laws are no good if they're not enforced, and if they're not enforced equally, we know that governments which fear religion can be quite oppressive, but we know that societies which think there's only one religion can be equally oppressive.

Now, the fact is that no matter how strongly each of us believes, none of us has the benefit of knowing all the truth that God holds in his hands. And therefore, we are doing the best we can here on earth to reflect and to give honor to our creator in a way that is manifest in our religious values. Because truly, at the root of every major religion, is a connection with the divinity, is an acceptance, and is a recognition that we all are walking a path together.

Now I know that some in my country and elsewhere have criticized this meeting and our work with all of you. But I want to make clear that I am proud of this work, and I am proud to be working with every one of you. And I believe that this work is an affirmation of America's values, but equally important an affirmation of universal values. Because we nor – no country individually has a monopoly on the truth, and we will do better when we live in peace with each other, when we live with respect and humility, and listen to each other. And it is important that we recognize what we accomplished when this resolution ended 10 years of divisive debate where people were not listening to each other anymore.

Now we are. We're talking. We have to get past the idea that we can suppress religious minorities that we can restrict speech that we are smart enough that we can substitute our judgment for God's and determine who is or is not blaspheming. And by bringing countries from around the world here, we are affirming our common humanity and our common commitment to defend and promote fundamental rights.

Now these will not be easy conversations. When I was growing up, my parents said, "You should never talk about religion, because you will always spark a fight." And that was even amongst people of the same faith. We have – there's lots of funny stories about different kinds of Christians that won't talk to other kinds of Christians, because another kind of Christian is not as good as the first kind of Christian. Well, we know that those kind of divisions exist in every major religion, where people claim that your particular version of religion is the only one that can be followed.

But people of all faiths have so much to gain by working together. And I was so moved by the images that we saw coming out of Tahrir Square back in February – January and February, where you saw Coptic Egyptians joining hands to form a protective circle around their Muslim brothers and sisters so they could pray safely in the midst of these huge crowds. And then you saw Muslims doing the same for their Christian brothers and sisters. That is, to me, the highest expression of religious tolerance and free expression that one could possibly find. Those were defining moments in 2011 and those are images that inspire me as we move into 2012.

So thank you. And I think interfaith dialogue, reaching out to those with whom you disagree, even agreeing to disagree, so to speak, is a part of the work we are struggling to do. And we can make progress where we have a new attitude in our world where we can believe strongly what we believe. We can think others are wrong, but we don't feel so insecure and so fearful of their wrong views that we try to suppress them, imprison them, or even kill them. Instead, we trust that over time, if they are wrong, they will come to see the error of their ways. But we continue the conversation as fellow human beings and as people of faith.

So I thank you very much for being with us, and I wish you well as you continue this absolutely important work. I think if we do our work right, in years to come, people will look back and say this was a great step forward on behalf of both freedom of religion, freedom of expression, and our common humanity. Thank you all very much.

Remarks by Ambassador-at-Large for International Religious Freedom Suzan Johnson-Cook, December 12, 2011

Good morning. Thank you all for coming here for what I hope will be the first in a series of meetings that will advance respect for religious freedom and religious tolerance around the world. I am Suzan Johnson Cook, the U.S. Ambassador at Large for International Religious Freedom, and I am honored to be your host for the next three days.

Before we begin, I would like to salute the many people, governments, and organizations here today who worked so hard to pass Human Rights Council Resolution 16/18, "Combating Intolerance, Negative Stereotyping and Stigmatization Of, and Discrimination, Incitement to Violence, and Violence Against Persons Based on Religion or Belief." That historic resolution was adopted by consensus in Geneva in March. As Secretary Clinton said in Istanbul in July, by passing it, "We have begun to overcome the false divide that pits religious sensitivities against freedom of expression."

The international community reinforced the spirit of Resolution 16/18 at the UN General Assembly, where the UNGA Third Committee adopted a similar resolution by consensus. I want to thank all of those who made that breakthrough possible, especially the Ambassadors from Geneva and New York who are with us here today.

Resolution 16/18 secured an international consensus around an action-oriented approach to combat religious intolerance in line with respect for universal human rights—including religious freedom and freedom of expression.

The resolution calls on states to take specific measures to combat religious intolerance. The focus of this implementation meeting is identifying best practices on prohibiting discrimination against individuals based on religion or belief, training government officials to avoid discrimination in their official duties, putting enforcement mechanisms in place and engaging with members of religious communities.

It is important that experts like you, practitioners of human rights protection, law enforcement, and community relations, share your views and exchange information on how to protect religious minorities.

You represent over 30 countries and a wide range of international organizations, including the European Union, the UN Office of the High Commissioner for Human Rights, the Organization for Security and Cooperation in Europe, and the Organization of Islamic Cooperation. With this kind of expertise, we can make progress on implementing this resolution. History will judge us not by the resolutions we pass – but by whether we put these resolutions into practice. As the famous American abolitionist Wendell Phillips once remarked, "Governments exist for the purpose of protecting the rights of minorities." Those rights include the right to believe and the right practice a religion not sanctioned by the state -- or no religion at all.
Though we come from a wide range of backgrounds, this resolution, representing the consensus of the international community, unites us in a common purpose. This purpose is to advance religious freedom, promote religious tolerance, and combat discrimination on the basis of

religion or belief—consistent with universal human rights principles. This means a commitment to protect religious minorities and protect freedom of expression. Fighting discrimination and improving respect for religious freedom also creates a climate of tolerance that promotes stability, social harmony, and security.

We know that some people distort various religious doctrines to justify intolerance, foment violence, or create strife that serves their narrow political purposes. We must denounce offensive speech whenever we encounter it – but our commitment to universal principles makes clear that faith must never be a crime and religion must never be used as an excuse to stifle freedom of expression.

Secretary Clinton put it this way in a February speech on Internet freedom: "Some take the view that, to encourage tolerance, some hateful ideas must be silenced by governments. We believe that efforts to curb the content of speech rarely succeed and often become an excuse to violate freedom of expression. Instead, as it has historically been proven time and time again, the better answer to offensive speech is more speech. People can and should speak out against intolerance and hatred. By exposing ideas to debate, those with merit tend to be strengthened, while weak and false ideas tend to fade away; perhaps not instantly, but eventually."

In this country, religious freedom is guaranteed in our Constitution's Bill of Rights. We continue to work at improving respect for our religious diversity and protecting freedom of expression. Yet we continue to see individuals involved in acts of intolerance, and attempts to discriminate against other religious groups. They usually get wide coverage in our free press, and yet, we have freedom of expression and use effective measures to deal with these issues that are consistent with the steps recommended in Resolution 16/18. Complacency is not an option.

Over the next three days, we seek frank discussions that will help our governments promote tolerance, combat discrimination and violence, and help us learn from each others' experiences. Resolution 16/18 is a roadmap. Our agenda for the next three days is to explore how to use that map to implement the resolution in ways that will improve conditions for all of our citizens.

Today, we will hold plenary sessions where you will meet your counterparts from the U.S. Department of Homeland Security and Department of Justice. They will share with you how our approaches to these problems are evolving, what we have adopted from other countries, and how we adapted based on experience. On Tuesday and Wednesday, our meetings will be divided into two tracks. The first track will explore effective government strategies to engage religious minorities. This discussion will include methods for training government officials on religious and cultural awareness. The second track will explore ways to better enforce laws that prohibit discrimination on the basis of religion or belief. We urge members of your delegation to participate in both tracks to ensure that we capture the full range of opinions and ideas you all represent.

Following this conference, we will compile a set of best practices that will be submitted to the Office of the High Commissioner of Human Rights to be shared with States and the general public.

This is a historic opportunity for all of our countries to make concrete advances in promoting tolerance and combating the discrimination and violence that blights so many lives. I welcome you to Washington as together we find ways to promote mutual respect between governments and citizens of all religions, creeds, and beliefs. Thank you.

Remarks by Assistant Attorney General Thomas E. Perez, Monday, December 12, 2011

I am very pleased and honored that my colleagues at the State Department invited me to speak to you at the opening of this three-day conference on combating discrimination and violence based on religion or belief. And it is a particular honor to address such a distinguished group of experts from nations around the world on this critically important subject.

The freedom of religious expression and worship, and the importance of being freed from discrimination and violence based on religion, are, as Secretary Clinton said, "Fundamental freedoms that belong to all people in all places." In the United States we sometimes call religious freedom "the First Freedom," because it was so important to the history of our nation's founding as a place where people of many different faiths could come and worship in peace, and because it is the first right listed in our Constitution's Bill of Rights.

The "First Freedom" phrase also acknowledges that religious freedom is a core right, involving our greatest aspirations and hopes as individuals, our central and defining beliefs, and the traditions and values that connect us to our predecessors and which we want to pass on to our children. This is why it is among the human rights and fundamental freedoms set forth in the Universal Declaration of Human Rights, Article 18 of which, as you know, states "Everyone has the right to freedom of thought, conscience and religion; this right includes freedom to change his religion or belief, and freedom, either alone or in community with others and in public or private, to manifest his religion or belief in teaching, practice, worship and observance."

The United Nations Human Rights Council echoed the Universal Declaration in resolution 16/18, which is the basis for this conference. As important as it is to assert such principles, however, it is equally or even more important to ensure that such principles are put into practice.

The United States' Declaration of Independence declared in 1776 that "all men are created equal," but it took 100 years and a civil war that took hundreds of thousands of lives to end slavery; another hundred years to create legal equality for African Americans; and we struggle to this day to make equality a reality. I see this every day in my work as the chief civil rights law enforcement official for the United States. I know first-hand the hard work that is involved and the frustrations when we fall short of our principles.

The same is true for religious freedom in the United States: we possess strong and timeless principles of religious liberty, but ensuring that they are a reality for all requires great vigilance, effort, and perseverance. And as with the issue of race, there is often a great distance between principle and reality. After the 9/11 terrorist attacks, we saw a sharp rise in hate crimes and discrimination against Muslims and people mistaken as being Muslim, including Arabs, South Asians, and Sikhs, as some people among us pursued the twisted logic that an attack on innocents could be avenged by another attack on innocents who simply shared the same faith or ethnicity of the perpetrators. We also see how we fall short of principle in the hate-fueled vandalism and arson of synagogues, as well as churches, especially African American churches. Countering and prosecuting such acts and ensuring the endurance of our ideals takes great focus and sustained effort.

This is the challenge before each of you in the work you do in your respective countries: how to make the promise of religious freedom and ending religious violence and discrimination a reality. And it is the challenge before this conference for us to engage in a dialogue in which we all might learn from one another how to better assure that these noble principles and goals are realized in practice.

I would like to help kick off this dialogue by talking a little about the American experience in putting the principles of religious liberty and religious tolerance into practice. Many of the people who first came to America from Europe were fleeing persecution and seeking a place to practice their religion in peace. While most of these people belonged to various Christian sects, the principles of religious freedom that were laid down were intentionally written in universal terms.

Thomas Jefferson, who also wrote the Declaration of Independence, which I mentioned earlier, wrote the Virginia Statute on Religious Freedom, passed in 1786. This seminal document provided the framework for the First Amendment of the United States Constitution three years later. The Virginia Statute eliminated laws that had barred non-Christians from holding public office and enjoying other legal privileges, and swept away heresy laws that had outlawed dissent from certain Christian doctrines.

When the Virginia Statute was being debated, there was a move by some legislators to insert a reference to Jesus Christ. This effort was defeated. Thomas Jefferson remarked that he was pleased that this maneuver failed, because indeed it had been his specific intention to include "the Jew, the Gentile, the Christian, Mohamaden and Hindu" under the law's protections.

George Washington, the first United States President and the man after whom this city is named after, likewise repeatedly expressed that religious liberty was intended for all. He expressed this in a famous letter to a Jewish congregation in Newport, Rhode Island, saying that the United States welcomed people of all faiths to become citizens.

America was and remains a country that is majority Christian. And its culture is heavily Christian, as the Christmas decorations you will see around the city this month attest. But its government has never been Christian. The second United States president, John Adams signed a treaty with the Bay of Tunis in 1797, declaring that "the Government of the United States of America is not, in any sense, founded on the Christian religion" and "has no character of enmity against the laws, religion, or tranquility of Muslims." It further stated that "no pretext, arising from religious opinions, shall ever produce an interruption of the harmony existing between the two countries."

This attention to religious freedom, stated by our founding fathers and in our founding documents, has a long and proud history in application. At the time of the American Civil War, for example, Quakers were vilified for their pacifistic stance and imprisoned for failing to fight for the union. After an appeal by Quaker leaders directly to President Abraham Lincoln, he granted them the right of conscientious objection, and that has been honored in every war since. It is in wartime, when the stakes are so high, that true dedication to principle is tested. In the middle of World War II, with patriotic fervor at its highest, the Supreme Court ruled that

Jehovah's Witness children could not be forced to say the pledge of allegiance to the United States, a stunning victory for conscience. Our dedication to religious liberty in these and many other contexts has led to the United States becoming a place where a multiplicity of faiths have flourished—not just major faith groups like Christians, Muslims, Jews, Sikhs, Hindus, and Buddhists, but thousands of sects and subsects within major faith groups.

This is not to say that we have always been consistent in supporting religious liberty. It is hard to think today of Catholics in the United States being a persecuted and despised minority—they constitute more than 25% of the population in the United States and are powerful politically, culturally, and economically. But the experience of Catholics in the 20th Century has many parallels to the plight of Muslims today. Catholics were immigrants and outsiders to the mainstream culture, and were seen by many as following a strange religion that was bent on world domination, in particular the undermining of American democracy and imposition of a theocracy.

The violence and hatred that Catholics faced was completely at odds with our fundamental principles. In 1834, a mob near Boston, Massachusetts burned down a convent, convinced that something evil was going on inside. In 1844, riots broke out in Philadelphia when a rumor circulated that Catholics were trying to remove the Bible from the public schools, resulting in the burning of Catholic churches and seminaries. In a story showing the best of the American tradition, at St. Joseph's Catholic Church, a large group of Quakers gathered and surrounded the church, preventing the mobs from destroying it.

Other groups have been met at various times in our history with discrimination and violence, in the United States, including Jews, Mormons, and most recently Muslims. This was never due to a failure of our principles, which reflect universal and timeless values, but rather a failure of applying them consistently.

Ensuring the realization of these values requires the efforts of all three branches of government—the Congress, in enacting laws to protect against religious discrimination and religious violence; —the executive branch, in enforcing these laws; —and the judiciary, interpreting these laws and protecting constitutional principles.

America's legacy of racial discrimination has ironically aided us in protecting religious liberty. In 1964, after the sustained advocacy of civil rights leaders such as Martin Luther King, Jr., Congress passed sweeping civil rights legislation to protect against discrimination in a wide range of contexts, including employment, education, public accommodation.

The Civil Rights Act of 1964 empowered the Department of Justice to use its resources to enforce the Act's provisions. While the main purpose of the Act was to end racial discrimination, the law also barred discrimination based on national origin, sex, and religion. This law and others enacted over the years since, provide my agency, the Civil Rights Division of the Department of Justice, with powerful tools to combat religious discrimination and religion-based violence.

While race-motivated hate crimes remain the greatest problem we address, we also prosecute many cases of religion-based hate crimes, including attacks and threats against individuals and vandalism and arson of places of worship. Attacks on Jews and vandalism of synagogues remain a serious problem, driven by the persistence of organized neo-Nazi groups. After 9/11, as I mentioned earlier, we witnessed a sharp rise in hate crimes against Muslims, and those perceived to be Muslim, including Arabs, Sikhs and South Asians. This dropped off sharply the following year and continually dropped over subsequent years. Then in 2010 we saw an upturn, with a 50% increase in hate crimes against Muslims. My office is vigorously prosecuting these cases.

We are currently prosecuting a man in the State of Oregon for allegedly setting fire to a mosque last year. Earlier this year, we obtained a conviction of a man who set fire to playground equipment outside of a mosque in Texas. This hate-fueled violence will not be tolerated.

We are actively working to prevent discrimination in employment. My office is currently suing New York City for refusing to allow Sikh men and Muslim women working as bus and subway drivers to wear religious head-coverings with their uniforms. These cases can touch many different faith groups. Two years ago, we settled a similar case against the Washington, D.C. transit authority for refusing to allow a Pentecostal woman bus driver to wear a skirt instead of pants with her uniform, and refusing to allow two Muslim women to wear headscarves.

We also bring suits to prevent religious discrimination and harassment in public schools. Earlier this year we resolved a case in which Somali Muslim students in Minnesota had been subject to harassment by other students and disproportionate discipline from school administrators.

We also protect religious exercise by students in public schools. We successfully sued a school in the State of Oklahoma for refusing to allow a Muslim girl to wear a headscarf to school. We have won the right for Muslim students to gather during the lunch hour to pray, and similarly for Christian students to gather for Bible study during free periods.

We have also brought cases involving housing discrimination based on religion, religious discrimination in public accommodations such as restaurants, and in access to public facilities, such as winning the right of women wearing headscarves to enter county courthouses in the State of Georgia. My colleagues from the Justice Department will be talking about these cases in the roundtable discussions over the next three days.

One final area I would like to highlight is our work fighting for the ability of religious groups to buy property and build places of worship and religious schools. In the United States, as in many countries, local officials in cities and towns have great power in determining which types of buildings will be allowed in which neighborhoods. Unfortunately, this power is often used in arbitrary or discriminatory ways to deny permits to religious communities.

In response, in 2000, Congress unanimously passed a law called the Religious Land Use and Institutionalized Persons Act that prohibits discriminatory or arbitrary denial of permission to religious communities to build places of worship or religious schools. The law gives the religious groups the right to sue, but it also empowers the Department of Justice to bring suit.

We have used this law to require cities to allow the building of churches, mosques, synagogues, a Buddhist Temple, a Sikh Gurdwara, and various religious schools. One area where we have seen a particularly large number of cases in the last two years is mosque construction. We are investigating many such cases, and just this past September, we resolved two cases—one in Virginia and one in Georgia—in which mosques had been denied permits that had been routinely granted to Christian churches. Our investigation also uncovered evidence of overt anti-Muslim bias. I am happy to report that the court-supervised settlement in those cases will allow the mosques to be built, and also require numerous corrective measures for the city and county involved, including training on nondiscrimination law and new procedures.

So as you can see, I have a lot of work to do, putting United States principles of religious freedom into practice, just as each of you do in your countries. While every country has its own unique situations and challenges, we can learn much from each other. My hope is that each of us will come away from this conference with clearer insights into the challenges that other countries face, and, just as importantly, with a new perspective on the challenges we each face in our own countries.

Thank you.

www.ingramcontent.com/pod-product-compliance
Lightning Source LLC
Chambersburg PA
CBHW080630290526
45790CB00007B/3005